STUPID EMILIEN

S. T. MENDELSON

STEWART, TABORI & CHANG

NEW YORK

To my friend and mentor Harold Balikov

S. T. M.

Copyright © 1991 S. T. Mendelson

Design by Diana M. Jones

Published in 1991 by
Stewart, Tabori & Chang, Inc.
575 Broadway, New York, New York 10012

Library of Congress Cataloging-in-Publication Data
Mendelson, S. T.
Stupid Emilien / S. T. Mendelson.
p.   cm.
Summary: Relates how a Russian peasant known as Stupid Emilien
manages to outwit the Czar and marry his daughter.
ISBN 1-55670-213-2
[1. Fairy tales.   2. Soviet Union—Fiction.]   I. Title.
PZ8.M522St   1991
[E]—dc20   90-28780
                                                    CIP

Distributed in the U.S. by Workman Publishing,
708 Broadway, New York, New York 10003
Distributed in Canada by Canadian Manda Group,
P.O. Box 920 Station U, Toronto, Ontario M8Z 5P9
Distributed in all other territories by
Little, Brown and Company, International Division,
34 Beacon Street, Boston, Massachusetts 02108

Printed in Japan

10   9   8   7   6   5   4   3   2   1

STUPID
EMILIEN

Everyone thought Emilien was stupid.

He never did anything. All winter he sat on the stove,
all summer he sat on the roof.

He even refused his brothers when they invited him to come
with them to the big city to seek their fortunes. "Why would I
want to leave? I like my stove. I like my roof. I like my
village and my neighbors. What more do I need?"

Everyone called him Stupid Emilien, but maybe he
wasn't so stupid after all.

When the weather turned warm, Stupid Emilien moved
from the stove to the roof.

One very warm day, he saw an old babushka trudging home
carrying heavy buckets of water. "Oh," cried Stupid Emilien loudly,
"buckets fly home by yourselves!" Off they flew. The babushka
was amazed and she ran and told everyone in the village
about Stupid Emilien's magic powers.

The whole village turned out to see Stupid Emilien perform his magic.
Dolls and nutcrackers danced with the villagers while heroes of ancient legends
rode across the sky in glory. Stupid Emilien granted every wish—every wish but one.
The mayor of the village demanded to be made czar and Stupid Emilien refused.

Perhaps he was not so stupid after all.

Furious, the mayor ran all the way to the very gates of the czar's palace, spreading nasty, untrue stories about Stupid Emilien and his magic. By the time the stories reached the czar, they told of a terrible, giant monster who threatened to overthrow him. The czar was very unhappy.

The czarevna, which is what a princess is called when her father is a czar, was thrilled. At last, here was an adventure! She demanded that they go to see this terrible monster at once.

By the time the czar and czarevna reached Stupid Emilien's village, they were cranky and tired. Not only was there no monster to be found, there were no adoring crowds of villagers yelling, "God save the czar!" There was only one peasant sitting on a roof, reading a book.

"You there," bellowed the czar. "Rude peasant!
Bow down before me. I am your czar."

"You there," responded Stupid Emilien. "Czar! You are rude.
Fly home now!" And off he flew.

The czar tumbled through his bedroom window, which luckily had
been left open. He was not happy. In fact he felt rather silly, which
was a feeling he did not like at all. Issuing orders always made
him feel better, so he issued an order to the mayor
of Stupid Emilien's village:

That very night, the mayor was to put Stupid Emilien into a barrel
and throw the barrel into the sea. After that, the czar
felt much better.

The next morning, Stupid Emilien awoke feeling strange.
In no time at all he realized that he was no
longer on his roof but that somehow he'd gotten
himself into a barrel far out at sea.

Because Stupid Emilien was not so stupid after all, he guessed that the czar was behind this trick. After a moment of thought, he turned the barrel into a flying castle and set off in the direction of the czar's palace.

The czar and czarevna were busy arguing over whom she should marry.
The czarevna thought that all the kings and
princes she had met were too dull to marry. Just then,
Stupid Emilien's flying castle came into view.

The czar agreed to take the czarevna on his ship to get a
closer look at the flying castle. He couldn't imagine
who owned such a splendid castle, but perhaps
here was a prince the czarevna would not
find too boring to marry.

Stupid Emilien sent servants mounted on flying horses
to the czar's ship to invite him and his daughter to
dinner. The czarevna accepted the
invitation for both of them.

The czar and czarevna were treated to the most sumptuous feast they could ever have imagined, by the most gracious host either had ever met. The czarevna, however, did think there was something familiar about their host, and he certainly wasn't boring.

At the end of the feast, the czar raised his glass and asked, "Good sir, please tell me your name so I can thank you for this glorious meal."

Stupid Emilien replied, "Why, Rude Peasant, of course."

Immediately Stupid Emilien turned the flying castle back into a barrel. The czar, the czarevna, and the peasant all floated in the sea together. The czar was terrified and furious, but the czarevna was enjoying her adventure. "Father," she said, "this is the one I'll marry."

"Now, Czar," began Stupid Emilien, "I don't like being put in a barrel and thrown out to sea any more than you do. To make sure that you don't do anything like this to me again, and because I rather like the idea, I think I will marry your daughter."

What a great wedding! Everyone was happy. The czarevna was happy with Stupid Emilien and Stupid Emilien was happy with her.

The czar was happy that his daughter was happy—but the czar
thought there was something that could make him even happier.

"Stupid Emilien, my boy," the czar said, "you are so great and powerful, and now you are like a son to me, maybe you should be czar. It's not so very hard really.

"Take my crown, take my glory, take my czardom! Be a czar. But perhaps you could leave me just a little crown, a little glory, and a little power."

Stupid Emilien thought for a moment. "Czar, keep your crown. Keep your glory. Keep your czardom and your power. Why would I want to be czar? I like my stove. I like my roof. I like my village and my neighbors. What more do I need?"

After all, Stupid Emilien was not so stupid.

Stupid Emilien and the czarevna returned to the village,
where they lived happily ever after, on the stove in winter
and on the roof in summer.

Come to think of it, everyone lived happily ever after, except . . .

. . . the czar.